1995 Examination
Suggested Solutions

Contract Law

LLB

University of London
External Examinations
Solutions by E A Lichtenstein
BA, LLB, LLM

HLT Publications

HLT PUBLICATIONS
200 Greyhound Road, London W14 9RY

Examination Questions © The University of London 1995
Solutions © The HLT Group Ltd 1995

ISBN 0 7510 0619 X

British Library Cataloguing-in-Publication.

A CIP Catalogue record for this book is available from the British Library.

Printed and bound in Great Britain.

CONTENTS

Acknowledgement   v

Introduction   vii

Examination Paper   3

Suggested Solutions

    Question 1   11

    Question 2   17

    Question 3   23

    Question 4   29

    Question 5   35

    Question 6   41

    Question 7   47

ACKNOWLEDGEMENT

The questions used are taken from the University of London LLB (External) Degree examination paper and our thanks are extended to the University of London for the kind permission which has been given to us to use and publish the questions.

Caveat

The answers given are not approved or sanctioned by the University of London and are entirely our responsibility.

They are not intended as 'Model Answers', but rather as Suggested Solutions.

The answers have two fundamental purposes, namely:

a) To provide a detailed example of a suggested solution to examination questions, and

b) To assist students with their research into the subject and to further their understanding and appreciation of the subject.

Note

Please note that the solutions in this book were written in the year of the examination. They were appropriate solutions at the time of preparation, but students must note that certain caselaw and statutes may subsequently have changed.

INTRODUCTION

Why choose HLT publications?

Holborn College has earned an international reputation for the outstanding quality of its teaching, Textbooks, Casebooks and Suggested Solutions to past examination papers.

Our expertise is reflected in the outstanding results achieved by our students in the examinations conducted by the University of London LLB Honours Degree Programme for External Students, the Council of Legal Education, and by students in over 70 universities who use our publications.

Suggested Solutions

The Suggested Solutions series provides examples of full answers to the problems posed by examiners. The solutions are much more than answers achievable by a candidate under examination conditions. The opportunity has been taken, where appropriate, to develop themes, suggest alternatives and set out additional material providing further comprehensive topical coverage.

To aid comprehension and revision, the solutions are fuller than would be possible under examination conditions. It is important to keep in mind that at this level there almost certainly is more than just one approach in answering any given question.

We feel that in writing full opinion answers we can assist you with your research and further your understanding and appreciation of the law.

Notes on examination technique

Although the SUBSTANCE and SLANT of the answer changes according to the subject-matter of the question, the examining body and syllabus concerned, the TECHNIQUE of answering examination questions does not change.

You will not pass an examination if you do not know the substance of a course. You may pass if you do not know how to go about answering a question although this is doubtful. To do well and to guarantee success, however, it is necessary to learn the technique of answering problems properly. The following is a guide to acquiring that technique.

Time

All examinations permit only a limited time for papers to be completed. All papers require you to answer a certain number of questions in that time, and the questions, with some exceptions carry equal marks.

It follows from this that you should never spend a disproportionate amount of time on any question. When you have used up the amount of time allowed for any one question STOP and go on to the next question after an abrupt conclusion, if necessary. If you feel that you are running out of time, then complete your answer in note form. A useful way of ensuring that you do not over-run is to write down on a piece of scrap paper the time at which you should be starting each part of the paper. This can be done in the few minutes before the examination begins and it will help you to calm any nerves you may have.

Reading the question

It will not be often that you will be able to answer every question on an examination paper. Inevitably, there will be some areas in which you feel better prepared than others. You will prefer to answer the questions which deal with those areas, but you will never know how good the questions are unless you read the whole examination paper.

You should spend at least 10 MINUTES at the beginning of the examination reading the questions. Preferably, you should read them more than once. As you go through each question, make a brief note on the examination paper of any relevant cases and/or statutes that occur to you even if you think you may not answer that question: you may well be grateful for this note towards the end of the examination when you are tired and your memory begins to fail.

Re-reading the answers

Ideally, you should allow time to re-read your answers. This is rarely a pleasant process, but will ensure that you do not make any silly mistakes such as leaving out a 'not' when the negative is vital.

The structure of the answer

Almost all examination problems raise more than one legal issue that you are required to deal with. Your answer should:

Identify the issues raised by the question
This is of crucial importance and gives shape to the whole answer. It indicates to the examiner that you appreciate what he is asking you about.

This is at least as important as actually answering the questions of law raised by that issue.

The issues should be identified in the first paragraph of the answer.

Deal with those issues one by one as they arise in the course of the problem
This, of course, is the substance of the answer and where study and revision pays off.

If the answer to an issue turns on a provision of a statute, CITE that provision briefly, but do not quote it from any statute you may be permitted to bring into the examination hall
Having cited the provision, show how it is relevant to the question.

If there is no statute, or the meaning of the statute has been interpreted by the courts, CITE the relevant cases
'Citing cases' does not mean writing down the name of every case that happens to deal with the general topic with which you are concerned and then detailing all the facts you can think of.

You should cite only the most relevant cases – there may perhaps only be one. No more facts should be stated than are absolutely essential to establish the relevance of the case. If there is a relevant case, but you cannot remember its name, it is sufficient to refer to it as 'one decided case'.

Whenever a statute or case is cited, the title of statute or the name of the case should be underlined
This makes the examiner's job much easier because he can see at a glance whether the relevant material has been dealt with, and it will make him more disposed in your favour.

Having dealt with the relevant issues, summarise your conclusions in such a way that you answer the question
A question will often say at the end simply 'Advise A', or B, or C, etc. The advice will usually turn on the individual answers to a number of issues. The point made here is that the final paragraph should pull those individual answers together and actually give the advice required. For example, it may begin something like: 'The effect of the answer to the issues raised by this question is that one's advice to A is that ...'

Related to the previous paragraph, make sure at the end that you have answered the question

For example, if the question says 'Advise A', make sure that is what your answer does. If you are required to advise more than one party, make sure that you have dealt with all the parties that you are required to and no more.

Some general points

You should always try to get the examiner on your side. One method has already been mentioned – the underlining of case names, etc. There are also other ways as well.

Always write as neatly as you can. This is more easily done with ink than with a ball-point.

Avoid the use of violently coloured ink eg turquoise; this makes a paper difficult to read.

Space out your answers sensibly: leave a line between paragraphs. You can always get more paper. At the same time, try not to use so much paper that your answer book looks too formidable to mark. This is a question of personal judgment.

NEVER put in irrelevant material simply to show that you are clever. Irrelevance is not a virtue and time spent on it is time lost for other, relevant, answers.

EXAMINATION PAPER

UNIVERSITY OF LONDON
LLB EXAMINATIONS 1995
for External Students
INTERMEDIATE EXAMINATION (Scheme A)
and
FIRST AND SECOND YEAR EXAMINATIONS (Scheme B)
GRADUATE ENTRY LEVEL I (Route A)
GRADUATE ENTRY FIRST YEAR (Route B)

ELEMENTS OF THE LAW OF CONTRACT

Tuesday, 13 June: 10.00 am to 1.00 pm

Answer *FOUR* of the following SEVEN questions

1   On Monday, A wrote to B offering to buy B's picture painted by Augustus John for £25,000. On Tuesday, B replied by leaving a message on A's answerphone stating, 'I assume that you mean the painting of four sisters and I accept.' The painting was worth £20,000. In addition to the painting called 'Four Sisters' B owned another painting by Augustus John called 'Forbidden Fruit' (worth £30,000). It was 'Forbidden Fruit' to which A was referring in his letter. On Wednesday, A was told that B owned two paintings by Augustus John, played back his answerphone and sent a message by electronic mail, via internet, to B's number saying, 'I accept both at £50,000. Unless I hear from you within two days I will assume that they are mine. You need not bother to reply.' B replied by letter to A stating, 'I may be prepared to sell both.' However, this letter was lost in the post.

   Advise the parties. What difference, if any, would it make to your advice if (a) because of a computer fault B had not received A's electronic mail message, or (b) because of a transmission failure the electronic mail message was incomplete and all that B received was, 'I accept'?

2   'Consideration is an historic device which should be dispensed with in modern times. The present rules on compromises of claim, omissions and agreeing to perform an existing legal duty

are unsatisfactory. What is necessary is some evidence of an intention to be bound by a clear promise.'

Discuss.

3 a) 'For a misrepresentation incorporated subsequently into a contract there are three possible categories of remedies available which makes advising clients very difficult.'

Discuss.

   b) D was considering buying a rare piece of china from E (an antique dealer). C, a friend of E, said to D that the piece was genuine. This was not correct but the piece was a very good fake. D agreed to buy the china for £25,000. Subsequently, the fact that it was a fake came to light.

Advise D. What difference, if any, would it make to your advice if, alternatively, (i) the statement had been made by E; (ii) E was a private seller?

4 F, an experienced sailor, agreed to buy a boat from G for £22,000. Subsequently, the agreement entered into between F and G contained, inter alia, the following clauses:

   '(9) It is agreed that there is no undertaking of quality, fitness for purpose or of description.

   (10) It is agreed that there is no express or implied condition or warranty, express, statutory or otherwise, fundamental or otherwise in this contract of sale.'

Two months later, on the first occasion F took the boat out to sea, the boat proved not to be seaworthy and nearly sank. The members of F's family who were acting as crew were seriously frightened for their lives and H, F's 14-year-old daughter, was mentally ill for two years.

Advise F who wants to return the boat and recover the price he has paid. What difference, if any, would it make to your advice if the boat had sunk?

5 J had lived with his girlfriend K for three years. They each contributed 50 per cent of the council tax and shared the other household expenses equally. J offered to buy for £10,000 K's shares in Big Bank plc, which she had inherited from her father. They were worth £100,000 and J knew this. K agreed because she was afraid that if she did not agree J would leave her. L, J's brother, threatened to tell J that he and K had had an affair before K had started to live with J. L forced K to sign a guarantee for a loan which L was taking from a bank as his business was in difficulty. The guarantee was secured by a charge on the flat in which K and J lived and which K owned.

Advise K. What would be your advice on the following alternative assumptions: (a) J had left K threatening to publish intimate photographs which he had taken when they were living together; or (b) L had become insolvent and the bank were seeking to enforce the guarantee; or (c) when K had agreed to the sale and guarantee she was only seventeen years old?

6 'Illegality renders a contract unenforceable by either party.'
   Discuss.

7 On Monday, M advertised in a local newspaper, the Trecynon Mail, that he was offering a reward of £5,000 to anyone finding and recovering a rare breed of dog, answering to the name of 'Gin'. M had lost the animal while exercising it on a nearby mountain. The dog was estimated to be worth £25,000. On Wednesday, N saw the advertisement and bought special equipment costing £1,500 which he used to try to find the dog. On Tuesday, P, a shepherd, found the dog attacking his sheep. He caught the dog and on Friday brought it down to the town of Trecynon where he was told about the reward. He went immediately to M to claim it. On Thursday, M had placed a notice in the Trecynon shop saying that the reward was no longer on offer.

   Advise M. What difference, if any, would it make to your advice if (a) P, who had found the dog, was a local constable, or (b) Q, P's son, had seen the notice in the village shop but had not told P about it?

SUGGESTED SOLUTIONS

QUESTION 1

On Monday, A wrote to B offering to buy B's picture painted by Augustus John for £25,000. On Tuesday, B replied by leaving a message on A's answerphone stating, 'I assume that you mean the painting of four sisters and I accept.' The painting was worth £20,000. In addition to the painting called 'Four Sisters' B owned another painting by Augustus John called 'Forbidden Fruit' (worth £30,000). It was 'Forbidden Fruit' to which A was referring in his letter. On Wednesday, A was told that B owned two paintings by Augustus John, played back his answerphone and sent a message by electronic mail, via internet, to B's number saying, 'I accept both at £50,000. Unless I hear from you within two days I will assume that they are mine. You need not bother to reply.' B replied by letter to A stating, 'I may be prepared to sell both.' However, this letter was lost in the post.

Advise the parties. What difference, if any, would it make to your advice if (a) because of a computer fault B had not received A's electronic mail message, or (b) because of a transmission failure the electronic mail message was incomplete and all that B received was, 'I accept'?

SUGGESTED SOLUTION TO QUESTION 1

General Comment

This is a somewhat complex question. The predominant points for discussion are the rules relating to the formation of the contract by offer and acceptance. There is, however, one aspect of the problem which requires reference to the effect of mistake. The possible confusion which this problem might present can be overcome by examining, and dealing with, the sequence of events stage by stage.

Skeleton Solution

B's message on A's answerphone – whether it constitutes an acceptance (the question of mistake must be referred to here), a counter offer, or a request for information.

The nature of A's message by electronic mail – whether it constitutes an acceptance or a fresh offer: if a fresh offer, the effect of the attempt to construe silence as acceptance.

B's reply by letter – whether it is an acceptance and, if so, the relevance of the postal rule.

The consequences of (a) B not receiving A's electronic mail message, or (b) B only receiving the incomplete message.

Suggested Solution

It is assumed that the letter sent by A on the Monday constitutes a clear offer. There is an element of doubt on this point as there are two paintings by Augustus John, and it may be difficult to determine, objectively, to which painting the offer can be held to relate.

The reply by B, the message on A's answerphone, is termed an acceptance by B. It cannot, however, be effective as such. The offer was made for the painting 'Forbidden Fruit' and the acceptance relates to the painting 'Four Sisters'. The parties are clearly not ad idem as to the subject matter and the contract would be void for mistake: *Raffles* v *Wichelhaus* (1); *Scriven Bros & Co* v *Hindley & Co* (2).

It is, in any event, by no means clear that B's message could be construed as an acceptance. Treitel (3) defines an acceptance as 'a final and unqualified expression of assent to the terms of an offer'. It would not appear that the message falls within this definition. The message could be construed either as a counter-offer, or as a request for information. If it is a counter-offer the effect of it would be to destroy the original offer: *Hyde* v *Wrench* (4). It may be, however, that the message could be regarded merely as a request for information, which would not amount to a rejection of the offer: *Stevenson Jacques & Co* v *McLean* (5). The question of whether a communication is a counter-offer or a request for information depends on the intention of the parties, objectively ascertained. It is submitted that, as the message introduces a different subject matter, it must be regarded as a counter-offer, which A is free to accept or reject. Accordingly no contract has been concluded at this point.

On the Wednesday A's message by electronic mail is clearly not an acceptance of B's offer, but a fresh offer to buy both paintings. His use of the words 'I accept' do not contradict the interpretation of the message as an offer; a statement may be an offer although it is expressed to be an 'acceptance': *Bigg* v *Boyd Gibbins Ltd* (6). The remainder of the message clearly indicates that it was intended as an offer.

In this message A is attempting to impose silence as constituting acceptance. The general rule is that an offeror cannot do so: *Felthouse* v *Bindley* (7). Whilst the offeree would not be bound by silence, it is possible that the the offeror could be held to have waived communication and to be bound by the offeree's silence – see the discussion by Treitel (8). This possibility is discussed below.

What has now to be discussed is whether A's fresh offer has been accepted. Two points must be considered: whether B's letter constitutes an acceptance; and, if it does, whether the acceptance can be deemed to have been communicated.

B's reply – 'I may be prepared to sell both' – cannot, it is submitted, be regarded as 'a final and unqualified assent' as required by the quotation from Treitel referred to above. That being so, the question whether it has been communicated is an academic one. The problem does, however, require consideration of it.

When an acceptance is sent by post it may be deemed to have been communicated when the letter is posted. This is the effect of the postal rule established in *Adams* v *Lindsell* (9). It matters not that the letter is lost in the post: *Household Fire Insurance Co* v *Grant* (10). The postal rule will apply '[w]here the circumstances are such that it must have been within the contemplation of the parties that, according to the ordinary usages of mankind, the post might be used as a means of communicating the acceptance of an offer' per

Lord Herschell in *Henthorn* v *Fraser* (11). If B's letter had constituted an acceptance, it could be argued that it was deemed to have been communicated by the application of the postal rule. It would not avail A to maintain that, having made the offer by electronic mail, he did not anticipate an acceptance through the post, but an instantaneous one, as he did not require a reply at all. However, it has been suggested that B's letter was not an unequivocal acceptance of A's offer.

My conclusion thus far is that B is not bound by A's offer transmitted by electronic mail, because the rule is that silence cannot be imposed on the offeree: *Felthouse* v *Bindley*. It is, however, possible to argue – as Treitel does (see previous reference) – that this rule was developed for the protection of the offeree, and that there is no reason in principle why the offeror should not be bound; although, as Treitel concedes, this possibilty has been judicially doubted: *Fairline Shipping Corporation* v *Adamson* (12). In the absence, therefore, of clear supporting authority B could not be advised that he could hold A to the offer to buy both paintings.

At this stage I remain of the view that no contract has been concluded.

I am asked to consider two further possibilities: (a) that B had not received A's electronic mail message; and (b) that B received only the incomplete message.

With regard to the first situation it is trite law that an offer must be actually communicated; an acceptance in ignorance of the offer can have no effect. The position would then be that B's counter-offer on A's answerphone to sell the painting 'Four Sisters' had not been accepted by A, and that there had been no further communication between the parties since then. My advice would, in consequence, would be the same, that no contract had been concluded.

The second situation gives rise to more doubt. Here B receives a message which appears to be an acceptance of his counter-offer for the sale of of the painting 'Four Sisters' at £25,000. This clearly was not A's intention, but could it be objectively construed as such? The answer would seem to depend on whether A knew (or had the means of knowing) of the transmission failure. Having chosen to use electronic mail as a method of communication it is arguable that A should bear the risk of imperfect transmission. Moreover his use of the expression 'I accept' would lead a reasonable person to believe that the message was a response – and therefore an acceptance – of the counter-offer. I conclude, although not without doubt, in the absence of clear authority, that on the assumption that A knew, or should have known of the possibility of the transmission failure, a contract would have been concluded on the terms of B's counter-offer.

References

(1)   (1864) 2 H & C 906
(2)   [1913] 3 KB 564
(3)   *The Law of Contract* (9th ed), p16
(4)   (1840) 3 Beav 334
(5)   (1880) 5 QBD 346
(6)   [1971] 1 WLR 913
(7)   (1862) 11 CB(NS) 869
(8)   *The Law of Contract* (9th ed), p32
(9)   (1818) 1 B & Ald 681
(10)   (1879) 4 Ex D 216
(11)   [1892] 2 Ch 27
(12)   [1975] QB 180

QUESTION 2

'Consideration is an historic device which should be dispensed with in modern times. The present rules on compromises of claim, omissions and agreeing to perform an existing legal duty are unsatisfactory. What is necessary is some evidence of an intention to be bound by a clear promise.'

Discuss.

SUGGESTED SOLUTION TO QUESTION 2

General Comment

A pitfall to be avoided in this question is the temptation to write all one knows about the doctrine of consideration without a clear focus on the issues posed by the question. What is required is: a brief exposition of the nature of the doctrine; an examination of the rules referred to in the light of the decided cases; and an analysis of the purpose of the doctrine and the alternative means suggested for achieving this purpose.

Skeleton Solution

The nature of the doctrine.

The rules and decided cases on compromises of claim, omissions and promises to perform an existing legal duty.

Purpose of the doctrine of consideration and its possible achievement by 'evidence of an intention to be bound'.

Suggested Solution

The doctrine of consideration has been developed by English law in order to determine which agreements should be legally enforceable. The basis of the doctrine, in the traditional view, is the idea of reciprocity: the law, it is said, enforces bargains, not bare promises. The classic definition of the doctrine was expressed by Lush J in *Currie* v *Misa* (1):

> 'a valuable consideration in the sense of the law may consist either in some right, interest, profit or benefit accruing to the one party, or some forbearance, detriment, loss or responsibility given, suffered or undertaken by the other.'

The idea of reciprocity is also inherent in the definition given by Sir Frederick Pollock (2):

> 'An act or forbearance of one party, or the promise thereof, is the price for which the promise of the other is bought, and the promise thus given for value is enforceable.'

This definition was adopted by the House of Lords in Dunlop *Pneumatic Tyre Co Ltd* v *Selfridge & Co Ltd* (3).

Where a promise is exchanged for a performance, or where there has been a mutual exchange of promises, the traditional theory presents no difficulties. Where, however, consideration has been found in a forbearance, compromise or performance of an existing duty, the traditional theory becomes harder to justify. Treitel (4) states that the courts have regarded an act of forbearance as the consideration for a promise even though the promisor had not intended to secure it. He terms this practice 'invented consideration'.

The compromise of a claim, or a forbearance to sue on it, can constitute good consideration. A promise not to enforce a valid claim is clearly good consideration for a promise given in return, but a promise not to enforce a claim known to be invalid is not: *Jones* v *Ashburnham* (5). The rules on doubtful claims, or claims wrongly believed to be valid, are less satisfactory. In *Haigh* v *Brooks* (6) the consideration was the surrender of a document believed to be a guarantee which turned out to be of doubtful validity. A promise to abandon a claim, even though it is clearly bad in law, is good consideration if the promisor believes it to be valid: *Callisher* v *Bishhoffsheim* (7); *Miles* v *New Zealand Alford Estate Co* (8).

With regard to promises to perform an existing legal duty the present state of the law appears to be somewhat confused. Three types of legal duty present themselves for discussion: an existing public duty, that is one imposed by law; an existing contractual duty to the promisor; and an existing duty to a third party.

There is old authority to the effect that the performance of, or the promise to perform, an existing public duty is not good consideration: *Collins* v *Godefroy* (9). Lord Denning, however, has consistently held that the performance of, or the promise to perform, a duty imposed by law can constitute good consideration: see his judgments in *Ward* v *Byham* (10) and *Williams* v *Williams* (11).

The promise to perform an existing contractual duty was held not to constitute good consideration in *Stilk* v *Myrick* (12). But the scope of that early decision has been curtailed by the Court of Appeal in *Williams* v *Roffey Bros & Nicholls (Contractors) Ltd* (13), where it was held that a promise to perform an existing obligation can amount to good consideration provided that there are practical benefits to the promisee. In his judgment Glidewell LJ confined his statement of the law to cases involving the provision of work or the supply of services. In *Re Selectmove Ltd* (14) the Court of Appeal refused to extend the principle of the *Williams* case to an obligation to make payment. To do so, Peter Gibson LJ held, would leave the principle in *Foakes* v *Beer* (15) without any application.

It appears to be settled law that the promise to perform an existing duty to a third party can be good consideration. This has been held in the early cases of *Shadwell* v *Shadwell* (16) and *Scotson* v *Pegg* (17) and affirmed by the Privy Council in *New Zealand Shipping Co Ltd* v *AM Satterthwaite & Co Ltd (The Eurymedon)* (18) and *Pao On* v *Lau Yiu Long* (19).

The strict application of the rules of the doctrine of consideration with regard to part payment of a debt – the principle in *Foakes* v *Beer* – can lead to injustice, an injustice which equity has attempted to mitigate by the development of the doctrine of promissory estoppel, stemming from the judgment of Denning J in *Central London Property Trust Ltd* v *High Trees House Ltd* (20). But a discussion of the doctrine of promissory estoppel is beyond the scope of this question.

The purpose of the doctrine of consideration is to determine what promises should be legally enforceable. Clearly not all promises can be held to be so. In his essay 'Consideration a Restatement' (21) Professor Atiyah states that 'consideration means the reason for the enforcement of a promise, or, even more broadly, a reason for the recognition of an obligation'. Atiyah dismisses as 'nonsensical' the notion of abolition of the doctrine. If the doctrine of consideration was to be abandoned the courts would have to employ an alternative method of deciding what promises should be enforced. The question suggests that this could be evidence of intention to be bound by a clear promise. But it is questionable whether this would be a satisfactory alternative. It could lead to even more uncertainty.

References

(1)   (1875) LR 10 Ex 133
(2)   *Pollock on Contracts* (13th ed), p133
(3)   [1915] AC 847
(4)   *The Law of Contract* (9th ed), p67
(5)   (1804) 4 East 455
(6)   (1839) 10 A & E 309
(7)   (1870) LR 5 QB 449
(8)   (1886) 32 Ch D 266
(9)   (1831) B & Ald 950
(10)   [1956] 1 WLR 496
(11)   [1957] 1 WLR 148
(12)   (1809) 2 Camp 317

References (continued)

(13)   [1990] 2 WLR 1153
(14)   [1995] 2 All ER 531
(15)   (1884) 9 App Cas 605
(16)   (1860) 9 CBNS 159
(17)   (1861) 6 H & N 295
(18)   [1975] AC 154
(19)   [1980] AC 614
(20)   [1947] 1 KB 130
(21)   *Essays on Contract*, p241

QUESTION 3

a) 'For a misrepresentation incorporated subsequently into a contract there are three possible categories of remedies available which makes advising clients very difficult.'
   Discuss.

b) D was considering buying a rare piece of china from E (an antique dealer). C, a friend of E, said to D that the piece was genuine. This was not correct but the piece was a very good fake. D agreed to buy the china for £25,000. Subsequently, the fact that it was a fake came to light.
   Advise D. What difference, if any, would it make to your advice if, alternatively, (i) the statement had been made by E; (ii) E was a private seller?

SUGGESTED SOLUTION TO QUESTION 3

General Comment

Part (a) of the question self-evidently requires an exposition of the remedies available for misrepresentation and breach of contract. Part (b) raises a number of issues, which are summarised in the Skeleton Solution.

Skeleton Solution

a) The three possible remedies available: rescission for misrepresentation; rescission (or the right to terminate the contract) for breach; damages for misrepresentation and for breach of contract.

The effect of the incorporation of the misrepresentation into the contract – s1 Misrepresentation Act 1967.

The difficulty of deciding the basis on which to claim damages.

b) D's possible rights against E under the Sale of Goods Act 1979. The possibility of a claim by D against C for negligent misstatement.
The possible effect of mistake.

  i) The effect if the statement had been made by E; and alternatively,

  ii) the effect of E being a private seller.

Suggested Solution

a) A possible remedy for misrepresentation is rescission of the contract. This remedy is available whether the misrepresentation be fraudulent or innocent. Whilst this remedy may often prove adequate, the right to rescind may be barred in four circumstances:

  1. by affirmation of the contract, where the injured party knows that he has the right to rescind: *Long* v *Lloyd* (1); *Peyman* v *Lanjani* (2);

  2. where restitutio in integrun is not possible: *Clarke* v *Dickson* (3);

3. where third party rights have intervened: *Lewis* v *Averay* (4); and

4. by lapse of time: *Leaf* v *International Galleries* (5).

The remedy for breach of contract depends on the nature of the breach. If the breach is of a condition (or of an innominate term, which is treated as a breach of condition) the injured party may elect to treat the breach as a repudiation of the contract and terminate it. If the breach is only a breach of warranty (or treated as such) the injured party is confined to a remedy in damages.

A remedy in damages is always available for breach of contract. The availability of damages for misrepresentation is a more complex question, the answer to which depends on the nature of the misrepresentation. Damages for fraudulent misrepresentation are always available, but the difficulty of substantiating an allegation of fraud appears from the criteria set out by Lord Herschell in *Derry* v *Peek* (6). Damages for fraud are based on the tortious measure, but subject to the special rule that, where fraud is established, it is not open to the guilty party to assert that the loss was not reasonably foreseeable: *Doyle* v *Olby (Ironmongers) Ltd* (7).

Prior to the Misrepresentation Act 1967 damages were not available where the misrepresentation was not fraudulent, only a claim for indemnity: *Whittington* v *Seale-Hayne* (8). However, s2(1) of the Act now provides the possibility of a remedy in damages where the misrepresentation is not fraudulent, unless the person making the misrepresentation can discharge the burden of proof which the section imposes. It is now clear that the measure of damages under s2(1) is the tortious one and is the same as for fraud: *Royscott Trust* v *Rogerson* (9).

Where a misrepresentation is subsequently incorporated into a contract, prior to the Act there may have been a difficulty that the term of the contract was to be treated only as a breach of warranty, thus confining the injured party to a remedy in damages and barring the right to rescind. This bar has been removed by s1 of the Act.

A difficulty that remains in advising clients is whether to base a claim for damages in contract (for breach), or in tort (for misrepresentation). The purpose of an award of damages for breach of contract is to put the injured party in the position he would have been in if the contract had been performed. The purpose of an award of damages in tort is to put the injured party in the position he would have been in if the wrong had not been committed. Damages in tort would not compensate a plaintiff for loss of bargain. However, damages for fraud and under s2(1) of the Act are subject to the special rule mentioned above. Whether the contractual or the tortious measure of damages is more advantageous to a client depends on the particular circumstances.

b) On the first scenario presented in this problem E has not made any statement regarding the piece of china. There can be no question of his liability for misrepresentation. (It is not suggested that C was acting as E's agent.) As E was selling in the course of a business, however, he may have incurred liability to D under s14(2) Sale of Goods Act 1979 (as amended by the Sale and Supply of Goods Act 1994). Section 14(2) provides that there is an implied term that the goods are of satisfactory quality. Under s14(2A) of the Act (as amended):

> 'goods are of satisfactory quality if they meet the standard that a reasonable person would regard as satisfactory, taking account of any description of the goods, the price (if relevant) and all the other relevant circumstances.'

In the absence of fuller information it is not possible to say whether there has been a breach of the implied term.

Mention should be made of the possibility of C having incurred liability to D for a negligent misstatement under the principle of *Hedley Byrne & Co* v *Heller & Partners* (10). However, there is no suggestion of negligence on C's part, nor of any special relationship between C and D.

It may well be that the contract between D and E was concluded as a result of a mistake as to the quality of the china. It is not clear, however, whether the mistake was unilateral or common. Without further information this aspect cannot be usefully discussed.

Two further, alternative hypotheses remain to be examined.

If the statement had been made by E he would have incurred liability for misrepresentation. This would afford D the right of rescission, provided that right had not been barred, as set out above. Even if the misrepresentation were not fraudulent D may be entitled to damages, as it is difficult to see that E, as an antique dealer, could discharge the onus imposed on him by s2(1) Misrepresentation Act 1967. The remedy of damages for misrepresentation has been discussed in part (a) of this question.

If E was a private seller it would appear that D would be without a remedy. Section 14(2) Sale of Goods Act 1979 would not apply. The only avenue that D could explore would be the law relating to mistake. But, as previously suggested, there is insufficient information on this point.

References

(1)   [1958] 1 WLR 753
(2)   [1985] Ch 457
(3)   (1858) EB & B 148
(4)   [1972] 1 QB 198
(5)   [1950] 2 KB 86
(6)   (1889) 14 App Cas 337
(7)   [1969] 2 QB 574
(8)   (1900) 82 LT 49
(9)   [1991] 2 QB 297
(10)   [1964] AC 465

QUESTION 4

F, an experienced sailor, agreed to buy a boat from G for £22,000. Subsequently, the agreement entered into between F and G contained, inter alia, the following clauses:

'(9) It is agreed that there is no undertaking of quality, fitness for purpose or of description.

(10) It is agreed that there is no express or implied condition or warranty, express, statutory or otherwise, fundamental or otherwise in this contract of sale.'

Two months later, on the first occasion F took the boat out to sea, the boat proved not to be seaworthy and nearly sank. The members of F's family who were acting as crew were seriously frightened for their lives and H, F's 14-year-old daughter, was mentally ill for two years.

Advise F who wants to return the boat and recover the price he has paid. What difference, if any, would it make to your advice if the boat had sunk?

SUGGESTED SOLUTION TO QUESTION 4

General Comment

There is more than one issue in this question. The main focus of the problem is on exclusion clauses. But with regard to the injuries suffered by F's family, discussion is required of the rules relating to privity of contract and the question whether damages are recoverable for those injuries must also be considered.

Skeleton Solution

The effect of the exclusion clauses at common law.

The validity of the clauses under the Unfair Contract Terms Act 1977.

The position in relation to the contract of F's daughter and the other members of his family.

The recoverability of damages for the fright occasioned to F's family and for the mental illness of his daughter.

Suggested Solution

At common law for an exclusion clause to be effective it must be incorporated into the contract and the clause must cover the breach. If it is effective at common law, its validity must be examined under the provisions of the Unfair Contract Terms Act 1977. It is not necessary here to discuss incorporation as the problem states that the contract contains the clauses.

The contract is one of sale of goods. It is not stated whether or not G sold the boat in the course of a business. If he did, the fact that the boat was not seaworthy means that there were breaches of the implied terms (conditions in England, Wales and Northern Ireland) that the boat was of satisfactory quality under s14(2) of the Sale of Goods Act 1979 (as amended), and that it was fit for the purpose for which it was bought under s14(3) of the same Act. If G were a private seller these sections would not apply. However it is submitted that, at common law, a term must be implied into the contract that the boat was seaworthy, and that the implication would pass the 'officious bystander' test propounded by MacKinnon LJ in *Shirlaw* v *Southern Foundries (1926) Ltd* (1).

The next question to be considered is whether the exclusion clauses cover the breach. The law on this point is set out in the trilogy of House of Lords' decisions in *Suisse Atlantique Société D'Armament Maritime SA* v *NV Rotterdamsche Kolen Centrale* (2); *Photo Production Ltd* v *Securicor Transport Ltd* (3); and *George Mitchell (Chesterhall) Ltd* v *Finney Lock Seeds Ltd* (4). The principle that has been established is that whether an exclusion clause is applicable where there has been a fundamental breach of contract is one of the true construction of the contract.

Was the fact that the boat was not seaworthy a fundamental breach of contract? I am inclined to the view that there was a fundamental breach of contract, but in the absence of further information as to the condition of the boat and as to other relevant circumstances it is difficult to give a more definite answer. In any event it is submitted that the clauses, in particular clause (10) of the agreement, would cover the breach, even if it were fundamental.

One has next to consider the validity of the clauses under the Unfair Contract Terms Act (UCTA) 1977. The two possibilities have to dealt with: (1) that G was selling in the course of a business; and (2) that G was a private seller.

If G sold the boat in the course of a business then, as previously stated, the statutory implied terms would apply. As it can be assumed that F was dealing as a consumer, then by virtue of s6(2) UCTA 1977, the exclusion clauses would be totally ineffective. There having been breaches of conditions of the contract, F would be entitled to return the boat and recover the purchase price.

If G sold the boat as a private seller then, as the statutory implied terms would not be applicable, s6 would not afford F any protection. Nor could s3 UCTA 1977 be invoked, as that section would operate only if G were dealing in the course of a business. It should be noted that the Unfair Terms in Consumer Contracts Regulations would also not apply as Regulation 2(1) defines a seller as one who 'is acting for purposes relating to his business'. If G acted as a private seller, therefore, F would have no redress.

It also appears from the facts presented that members of F's family were seriously frightened and that F's 14-year-old daughter suffered mental illness. Whether they have contractual rights against G depends on two factors: (1) were they parties to the contract?; and (2) are damages recoverable for their distress?

In the light of *Jackson* v *Horizon Holidays Ltd* (5), as explained by Lord Wilberforce in *Woodar Investment Development Ltd* v *Wimpey Construction UK Ltd* (6), it could be argued that F, his daughter and the other members of his family were all parties to the contract or, alternatively, that any recoverable loss suffered by his family was also F's loss.

The next question is whether the fright sustained by the family and the mental illness suffered by F's daughter can be compensated by an award of damages. I must consider the circumstances in which damages for distress can be recovered.

The general rule is that damages are not recoverable for mental distress in an action for breach of contract: *Addis* v *Gramophone Co Ltd* (7). However, in *Watts* v *Morrow* (8) Bingham LJ stated as follows:

> 'But the rule is not absolute. Where the very object of a contract is to provide pleasure, relaxation, peace of mind ... damages will be awarded if the fruit of the contract is not provided or if the contrary result is procured instead.'

It follows that damages could be recoverable for the distress suffered by F's family. This, however, depends on whether the exclusion clauses are operative. If liability for breach of contract has been effectively excluded (if G were a private seller) then no liability can arise for the mental distress. Such liability could only arise if the exclusion clauses were held to be ineffective.

Lastly, I am asked to consider if my advice would be different if the boat had sunk.

I can only suggest possibilities. It may be that the sinking of the boat would be of such a serious, fundamental nature that the exclusion clauses could not be construed as covering the breach of contract. In this event G would incur liabilty for breach, even if he were a private seller. It may also be that the sinking of the boat would deprive F of the right to return it, and he would have to seek redress in damages.

References

(1)   [1939] 2 KB 206
(2)   [1967] 1 AC 361
(3)   [1980] AC 827
(4)   [1983] 2 AC 803
(5)   [1975] 1 WLR 1468
(6)   [1980] 1 WLR 277
(7)   [1909] AC 488
(8)   [1991] 1 WLR 1421

QUESTION 5

J had lived with his girlfriend K for three years. They each contributed 50 per cent of the council tax and shared the other household expenses equally. J offered to buy for £10,000 K's shares in Big Bank plc, which she had inherited from her father. They were worth £100,000 and J knew this. K agreed because she was afraid that if she did not agree J would leave her. L, J's brother, threatened to tell J that he and K had had an affair before K had started to live with J. L forced K to sign a guarantee for a loan which L was taking from a bank as his business was in difficulty. The guarantee was secured by a charge on the flat in which K and J lived and which K owned.

Advise K. What would be your advice on the following alternative assumptions: (a) J had left K threatening to publish intimate photographs which he had taken when they were living together; or (b) L had become insolvent and the bank were seeking to enforce the guarantee; or (c) when K had agreed to the sale and guarantee she was only seventeen years old?

SUGGESTED SOLUTION TO QUESTION 5

General Comment

The main part of this question raises issues of undue influence, both actual and presumed. On the alternative assumptions discussion is required of: duress; the position of the third party (the bank); and K's capacity to contract.

Skeleton Solution

A summary of the doctrine of undue influence; actual influence and presumed influence.

The sale of the shares – whether entered into under undue influence.

The signing of the guarantee – the nature of the influence.

The alternative assumptions:

a) the threat to publish the photographs – undue influence and duress considered;

b) the enforcement of the guarantee by the bank – the position of a third party;

c) the question of K's capacity to contract.

Suggested Solution

A person who has been induced to enter into a contract by the undue influence of another (the wrongdoer) is entitled to have that contract set aside as against the wrongdoer. Undue influence is either actual or presumed. The classification of undue influence adopted by the Court of Appeal in *Bank of Credit and Commerce International SA* v *Aboody* (1) and by the House of Lords in *Barclays Bank plc* v *O'Brien* (2) was on the following lines.

1. *Class 1: actual undue influence.* This involves actual pressure, and it is for the claimant to prove that the wrongdoer exerted the undue influence on the complainant to enter into the particular transaction.

2. *Class 2: presumed undue influence.* Where the complainant shows that there was a particular relationship of trust and confidence between the complainant and the wrongdoer, the presumption

35

will arise that the wrongdoer abused that relationship in inducing the complainant to enter into the transaction. In this class it is not necessary for the complainant to prove undue influence in relation to the particular transaction. Once the confidential relationship is established the burden then passes to the wrongdoer to rebut the presumption, by proving that the complainant entered into the transaction voluntarily.

3. *Class 2A: special relationships.* Certain relationships, such as solicitor and client, doctor and patient, will give rise to the presumption of undue influence.

4. *Class 2B: de facto relationships.* The presumption of undue influence will arise even in the absence of a special relationship if the complainant shows that there was a relationship of trust and confidence between the complainant and the wrongdoer.

The transactions into which K entered must be examined in the light of the above principles.

The sale of the shares to J
The relationship between J and K is one falling within Class 2B. Where there is an emotional relationship between cohabitees there is, as Lord Browne-Wilkinson said in *Barclays Bank plc v O'Brien*, an underlying risk of one cohabitee exploiting the emotional involvement and trust of the other. It seems clear, because of K's fear that J would leave her, and her agreeing to sell shares worth £100, 000 for £10,000, that a relationship of trust and confidence existed. In *Lloyd's Bank Ltd v Bundy* (3) Sir Eric Sachs said that the presumption of undue influence arises:

> 'where someone one relies on the guidance or advice of another, where the other is aware of that reliance and where the person on whom reliance is placed obtains, or may well obtain, a benefit from the transaction …'.

This approach was approved by the House of Lords in *National Westminster Bank plc v Morgan* (4). In the latter case it was also held that, where the presumption of undue influence arose, it was also necessary for the complainant to show that there was 'manifest disadvantage' to the complainant in the transaction. This again is clearly the position here.

The onus now falls on J to prove that K entered into the transaction voluntarily. The most usual way of doing this is to show that the complainant had independent advice. Whilst there is no invariable rule that independent advice is necessary, this may be the only means by which the presumption of undue influence can be rebutted: *Inche Noriah v Shaik Allie Bin Omar* (5).

It does not appear that K had independent advice, nor are any other circumstances suggested which would enable J to prove that K entered into the transaction voluntarily. Accordingly K would be entitled to set the transaction aside.

The signing of the guarantee on behalf of L
This situation falls within Class 1: actual undue influence. We are told that L forced K to sign the guarantee by his threat. Once actual influence has been established it is not necessary for K to show that the transaction was to her disadvantage: *CIBC Mortgages* v *Pitt* (6).

K could also have this transaction set aside.

It remains to consider the alternative assumptions.

a) *J's threat to publish the photographs*
Presumably J uttered this threat in order to induce K to sell him the shares. Although this is not clearly stated, it is difficult to see how it would be otherwise be relevant.

As the relationship between J and K has terminated, in the circumstances described, the presumption of undue influence cannot arise: there is no longer a relationship of trust and confidence. It would appear, however, that there has been actual influence, with the consequences set out above. Moreover, the threat raises the possibility of invoking the doctrine of duress. Duress involves the application of illegitimate pressure on the victim which gives the victim no real choice but to submit: *Universe Tankships of Monrovia* v *International Transport Workers' Federation (The Universe Sentinel)* (7). It is not clear that the threat to publish the photographs constitutes illegitimate pressure, but it is blackmail, and in *The Universe Sentinel* Lord Scarman stated that the doctrine of duress should extend to blackmail.

On this assumption, therefore, K would also be entitled to have the transaction set aside.

b) *The enforcement of the guarantee by the bank*
It has been submitted that the guarantee was executed as a result of the actual influence. The position of the bank depends on whether they had constructive notice of the actual influence. If the bank did, it would have had to take reasonable steps to satisfy itself that K had entered into the obligation freely and with knowledge of the true facts. Otherwise the bank will not be able to enforce the guarantee: *Barclays Bank plc* v *O'Brien* (above). If the bank could not be held to have had constructive notice of the actual influence, it would not be tainted by the wrong, and K would not be able to resist enforcement: *CIBC Mortgages* v *Pitt*.

c) *The situation if K was only 17 years old at the relevant times*
   As K was a minor at the the time she entered into the sale and
   the guarantee the transactions would not be binding on her. If,
   however, the shares had been transferred to J, she could not
   recover them merely by reason of her minority: *Corpe* v *Overston*
   (8).

References

(1)   [1990] 1 QB 923
(2)   [1994] 1 AC 180
(3)   [1975] QB 326
(4)   [1985] AC 686
(5)   [1929] AC 127
(6)   [1994] 1 AC 200
(7)   [1983] 1 AC 366
(8)   (1833) 10 Bing 252

QUESTION 6

'Illegality renders a contract unenforceable by either party.'
   Discuss.

SUGGESTED SOLUTION TO QUESTION 6

General Comment

This is a straightforward single-issue question. It requires discussion of the positions of the guilty and the innocent parties to an illegal contract.

Skeleton Solution

Enforcement by the guilty party.

A wrong independent of the illegal contract.

A contract illegally performed.

Enforcement by the innocent party.

Alternative remedies available to the innocent party.

Suggested Solution

In discussing the enforceability of illegal contracts it is necessary to consider the respective positions of the guilty and the innocent parties.

The guilty party

The general rule is that the guilty party, that is one who knew of the illegality, cannot enforce an illegal contract: *Pearce* v *Brooks* (1).

Whilst the guilty party cannot enforce an illegal contract, he is not debarred from bringing an action on a wrong *independent* of the illegal contract. Thus in *Edler* v *Auerbach* (2) the landlord succeeded in a claim in tort in respect of a bath wrongfully removed by the tenant of premises let under an illegal lease.

Where the illegality lies in the method of performance, the guilty party may be able to enforce it. The shipowner in *St John Shipping Corporation* v *Joseph Rank Ltd* (3) successfully claimed his freight charges although he had overloaded his ship, contrary to statute. In *Howard* v *Shirlstar Container Transport Ltd* (4) the defendants engaged the plaintiff to fly aircraft, which they owned, out of Nigeria for a fee. The plaintiff in doing so committed breaches of Nigerian air traffic control regulations. It was held that this did not debar him from claiming his fee. The basis of that decision was that 'it would not amount to an affront to the public conscience to afford the plaintiff the relief he sought'. This 'public conscience' test was, however, rejected by the House of Lords in *Tinsley* v *Milligan* (5). The House of Lords held that the purpose of the legislation in *Howard* as in *St John Shipping* was not to invalidate contracts but only to prohibit conduct.

The contract would not be enforceable where the intention that one party should do an illegal act existed at the time of contracting: *Ashmore, Benson, Pease & Co Ltd* v *A V Dawson Ltd* (6).

The innocent party

A party to an illegal contract may be innocent, because he is mistaken either as to the law or as to the facts.

The general rule is that mistake of law does not give the innocent party the right to enforce the contract: *Nash* v *Stevenson Transport Ltd* (7).

Where a party is mistaken as to the facts he *may* be able to enforce it. There are cases where a claim by an innocent party has been upheld, and cases where the claim has been rejected.

In *Archbolds (Freightage) Ltd* v *S Spanglett Ltd* (8) the defendants contracted to carry the plaintiffs' whisky in a van which was not licensed to carry goods belonging to third parties, thus committing a statutory offence. The whisky was stolen, and the plaintiffs, who did not know that the van was not properly licensed, were able to recover damages for breach of contract.

A leading case where the claim of the innocent party was rejected is that of *Re Mahmoud and Ispahani* (9). A contract was made to sell linseed oil. At that time it was an offence, by legislation, to buy or sell linseed oil without a licence. The seller had a licence to sell and was induced to enter into the contract by the buyer's fraudulent misrepresentation that he also had a licence. The buyer later refused to accept the oil and it was held that the seller could not claim damages for non-acceptance.

The tests upon which to decide whether an illegal contract should or should not be enforceable are not entirely clear. One suggestion is that the innocent party can sue if the contract is illegal as performed, but not where it is illegal in its formation. This appears to be the approach in Cheshire, Fifoot and Furmston's *Law of Contract* (10). But Treitel (11) observes that this does not fit all the cases.

With regard to statutory prohibitions, the principles on which it should be decided whether an innocent party's claim should be accepted or rejected were set out by Kerr LJ in *Phoenix General Insurance Co of Greece SA* v *Administration Asigurarilor de Stat* (12). His Lordship held that where a statute prohibits both parties from concluding or performing a contract when both or either of them have no authority to do so, the contract is impliedly prohibited. But where a statute merely prohibits one party from entering into a contract and/or imposes a penalty on him if he does so, it does not follow that the contract itself is impliedly prohibited. Whether or not the statute has this effect depends on considerations of public policy.

Even if the innocent party is not able to enforce the contract he may have alternative remedies. He may have an action on a collateral contract or a claim based on misrepresentation.

In *Strongman (1945) Ltd* v *Sincock* (13) the defendant employed a firm of builders to effect work on his house. He promised to obtain the necessary licences, without which it was illegal to do the work. He only got licences for part of the work. The builders could not sue on the building contract, which was illegal, but recovered damages for breach of the collateral undertaking to obtain the necessary licences.

In *Shelley* v *Paddock* (14) the plaintiff was induced by the fraudulent misrepresentation of the defendant to enter into a contract to buy a house in Spain. This involved a violation of exchange control regulations. As the plaintiff's breach of the law was innocent, she was entitled to damages for the fraud.

References

(1) (1866) LR 1 Ex 213
(2) [1950] 1 KB 359
(3) [1957] 1 QB 267
(4) [1990] 1 WLR 1292
(5) [1994] 1 AC 340
(6) [1973] 1 WLR 828
(7) [1936] 2 KB 128
(8) [1961] 1 QB 374
(9) [1921] 2 KB 716
(10) (12th ed), pp 375, 388
(11) *Law of Contract* (9th ed), p444
(12) [1988] QB 216
(13) [1955] 2 QB 525
(14) [1980] QB 348

On Monday, M advertised in a local newspaper, the Trecynon Mail, that he was offering a reward of £5,000 to anyone finding and recovering a rare breed of dog, answering to the name of 'Gin'. M had lost the animal while exercising it on a nearby mountain. The dog was estimated to be worth £25,000. On Wednesday, N saw the advertisement and bought special equipment costing £1,500 which he used to try to find the dog. On Tuesday, P, a shepherd, found the dog attacking his sheep. He caught the dog and on Friday brought it down to the town of Trecynon where he was told about the reward. He went immediately to M to claim it. On Thursday, M had placed a notice in the Trecynon shop saying that the reward was no longer on offer.

Advise M. What difference, if any, would it make to your advice if (a) P, who had found the dog, was a local constable, or (b) Q, P's son, had seen the notice in the village shop but had not told P about it?

SUGGESTED SOLUTION TO QUESTION 7

General Comment

This is a further question involving discussion of the rules relating to offer and acceptance, although a different aspect. The main focus for discussion is the offer of a reward, the revocation of the offer and whether or not the offer had been accepted. Reference is also required to the sufficiency of consideration in the context of the performance of an existing public duty. Thus there is some overlap of subject matter between this question and both questions 1 and 2.

Skeleton Solution

The advertising of the reward – the nature and effect of unilateral offers.

The revocation of the offer – whether effectively communicated.

The rights of N in relation to the offer.

P's rights in relation to the offer.

The position if:

a) P was a local constable;

b) Q had seen the notice in the village shop, but had not informed P.

Suggested Solution

The advertising of the reward constitutes a unilateral offer 'made to all the world which is to ripen into a contract with anybody who comes forward and performs the conditions': *Carlill* v *Carbolic Smoke Ball Co* (1); *New Zealand Shipping Co Ltd* v *AM Satterthwaite & Co Ltd (The Eurymedon)* (2).

The acceptance of the offer would be the 'finding and recovering' of the dog.

An offer can be revoked at any time before acceptance: *Routledge* v *Grant* (3). In order, however, for a revocation to be effective, it must be communictaed to the offeree before the offer has been accepted: *Byrne* v *Van Tienhoven* (4).

M, having advertised the offer of the reward in the local newspaper, has purported to revoke the offer by a notice in the shop. It is extremely doubtful whether this constitutes an effective revocation. In *Shuey* v *United States* (5) the offer had been made in a newspaper publication and the revocation published in the same newspaper. The Supreme Court of the United States held that the revocation of an offer of a reward was effective where:

> 'it was withdrawn through the same channel in which it was made. The same notoriety was given to the revocation that was given to the offer ...'.

This cannot be said of the purported revocation in this problem. It is submitted, therefore, that the placing of the notice in the shop did not constitute an effective revocation.

The rights of N in relation to the offer

N had bought special equipment which he used trying to find the dog. Clearly he would not be entitled to the reward until he had fully performed the condition required. But it could be argued that N had accepted the offer by embarking on performance. In *Daulia* v *Four Millbank Nominees* (6) Goff LJ said that:

> 'there must be an implied obligation on the part of the offeror not to prevent the condition becoming satisfied, which obligation it seems to me must arise as soon as the offeree starts to perform.'

A similar approach was adopted by the Court of Appeal in *Errington* v *Errington and Woods* (7). It has been submitted that the placing of the notice in the shop did not constitute an effective revocation, but in any event N had started performance before M had placed the notice.

If there is the obligation not to revoke the offer once the offeree has commenced performance, M's purported revocation is a breach of contract, entitling N to sue for damages. It appears that the equipment N had bought cost £1,500. Damages in this amount may not be too remote given the worth of the dog. But insufficient information is given in the question to assess the quantum of damages.

The rights of P in relation to the offer

When P found the dog he was unaware of the offer. Indeed he was unaware of the offer until after he had brought the dog down to the town. It is clear that if the offeree is unaware of the offer he is not entitled to the reward, even though he performs the required condition: *R* v *Clarke* (8). Here, however, it appears that P informed M that he had recovered the dog after learning of the reward. It is possible that the decision in *Gibbons* v *Proctor* (9) could be applied so as to entitle P to the reward. If this were so, and it is by no means certain that it is, P's claim for the reward would not be defeated by the fact that he caught the dog because it was attacking his sheep. This may have been the motive for his catching the dog, but this would not be relevant if he was held to have acted within the terms of the offer: *Williams* v *Carwardine* (10).

I am asked to consider my advice if: (a) P, who had found the dog, was a local constable; or (b) Q, P's son had seen the notice in the shop but had not told P about it.

a) *If P was a local constable*

In this situation P, in finding and recovering the dog, could be held to have acted in the discharge of a public duty. On the strict application of *Collins* v *Godefroy* (11) P would not have furnished good consideration for the promise. But this case has come under scrutiny: see *Ward* v *Byham* (12); *Williams* v *Williams* (13); and *Williams* v *Roffey Bros & Nicholls (Contractors) Ltd* (14). In the light of these later developments and as there would not appear to be any public policy reasons to the contrary, I consider that, as P has conferred a factual benefit on M, there is good consideration for the promise. Therefore the mere fact that P was a local constable should not disentitle him to the reward.

b) *If Q had not told P about the notice*

I am not at all sure what is required here. It might be suggested that P was deemed to have knowledge of the revocation because his son could have been expected to tell him of it. Alternatively, the fact that Q saw the notice implies that there was adequate notice of the revocation of the offer. But these are slender suppositions and would not affect my advice.

References

(1)   [1893] 1 QB 256
(2)   [1976] AC 154
(3)   (1828) 4 Bing 653
(4)   (1880) 5 CPD 344
(5)   (1875) 92 US 73
(6)   [1978] 2 WLR 621
(7)   [1952] 1 KB 290
(8)   (1927) 40 CLR 227
(9)   (1891) 64 LT 594
(10)   (1853) 5 C & P 566
(11)   (1831) B & Ald 956
(12)   [1956] 1 WLR 496
(13)   [1957] 1 WLR 148
(14)   [1990] 2 WLR 1153

HLT Publications

HLT books are specially planned and written to help you in every stage of your studies. Each of the wide range of textbooks is brought up-to-date annually, and the companion volumes of our Law Series are all designed to work together.

You can buy HLT books from your local bookshop, or in case of difficulty, order direct using this form.

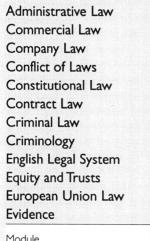

The Law Series covers the following modules:

Administrative Law	Family Law
Commercial Law	Jurisprudence
Company Law	Land Law
Conflict of Laws	Law of International Trade
Constitutional Law	Legal Skills and System
Contract Law	Public International Law
Criminal Law	Revenue Law*
Criminology	Succession
English Legal System	Tort
Equity and Trusts	
European Union Law	*No Textbook or Casebook
Evidence	available for this title

The HLT Law Series:

A comprehensive range of books for your law course, and the legal aspects of business and commercial studies.

Each module is covered by a comprehensive six-part set of books

- Textbook
- Casebook
- Revision Workbook
- Suggested Solutions, for:
  - 1985-90
  - 1991-94
  - 1995

Module	Books required	Cost

To complete your order, please fill in the form overleaf

Postage	
TOTAL	

Prices (including postage and packing in the UK): Textbooks £19.00; Casebooks £19.00; Revision Workbooks £10.00; Suggested Solutions (1985-90) £9.00, Suggested Solutions (1991-94) £6.00, Suggested Solutions (1995) £3.00.

For Europe, add 15% postage and packing (£20 maximum). For the rest of the world, add 40% for airmail (£35 maximum).

ORDERING

By telephone to 01892 724371, with your credit card to hand

By fax to 01892 724206 (giving your credit card details).

By post to:

HLT Publications,
The Gatehouse, Ruck Lane, Horsmonden, Tonbridge, Kent TN12 8EA

When ordering by post, please enclose full payment by cheque or banker's draft, or complete the credit card details below.

We aim to despatch your books within 3 working days of receiving your order.

Name

Address

Postcode

Telephone

Total value of order, including postage: £ _____

I enclose a cheque/banker's draft for the above sum, or

charge my ☐ Access/Mastercard   ☐ Visa   ☐ American Express

Card number

Expiry date

Signature

Date

Publications from **The Old Bailey Press**

Cracknell's Statutes

A full understanding of statute law is vital for any student, and this series presents the original wording of legislation, together with any amendments and substitutions and the sources of these changes.

Cracknell's Companions

Recognised as invaluable study aids since their introduction in 1961, this series summarises all the most important court decisions and acts, and features a glossary of Latin words, as well as full indexing.

Please telephone our Order Hotline on 01892 724371, or write to our order department, for full details of these series.